REAL ESTATE INVESTING SECRETS

A No-B.S. Guide to Creating Wealth & Freedom

MELANIE & DAVE DUPUIS

**Real Estate Investing Secrets:
A No-B.S. Guide to Creating Wealth & Freedom**
Published by Dupuis Publishing
Copyright © 2019 by Melanie & Dave Dupuis

All rights reserved.

No part of this publication may be reproduced, distributed, or transmitted in any form or by any means, including photocopying, recording, or other electronic or mechanical methods, without the prior written permission of the publisher, except in the case of brief quotations embodied in critical reviews and certain other noncommercial uses permitted by copyright law. For permission requests, write to the publisher, addressed "Attention: Permissions Coordinator," at the address below.

Dupuis Publishing
1385 Cassells St. North Bay, ON P1B 4B9

Limit of Liability/Disclaimer of Warranty:

While the publisher and author have used their best efforts in preparing this book, they make no representations or warranties with respect to the accuracy or completeness of the contents of this book and specifically disclaim any implied warranties of merchantability or fitness for a particular purpose. No warranty may be created or extended by sales representatives or written sales materials. Neither the publisher nor author shall be liable for any loss of profit or any other commercial damages, including but not limited to special, incidental, consequential, or other damages.

Publishing and editorial team: Author Bridge Media,
www.AuthorBridgeMedia.com
Project Manager and Editorial Director: Helen Chang
Editor: Jenny Shipley
Publishing Manager: Laurie Aranda
Cover Design: Iskon Design

ISBN: 978-1-9995464-0-3 -- paperback
978-1-9995464-1-0 -- ebook

Ordering Information:

Quantity sales. Special discounts are available on quantity purchases by corporations, associations, and others. For details, contact the publisher at the address above.

Printed in Canada.

DEDICATION

We dedicate this book with much love to three precious children: Kaitlyn Thomas, Amy Thomas, and Kolton Dupuis.

Mom and Dave/Dad had a huge wake-up call after the horrific highway roll-over crash. Although we were doing well, we didn't have as much freedom in our lives as we wanted. We don't want you to make the same mistake we did and wait for a near-death experience to live the life you want to live. Just light that fire under you, believe in yourself, take action, and create! If you don't know how you're going to do something or don't know the answers, don't waste time worrying and most importantly don't let that stop you. Just start, and you'll figure it out along the way. Once you start doing this, you'll see how easy the problem-solving process is and you'll gain confidence to know that you can overcome anything. Don't let anyone stand in the way of what you want or let others convince you otherwise. You absolutely can achieve all your dreams!

Remember our old blue rusted minivan that would squeal so loudly every time we started it? How about when we lived in the small two-bedroom apartment on Morin St. with the paper-thin windows when Mom was pregnant with Kolton? We sacrificed short term so we can live the life we want to live in the long term. Reflecting back at that time, our goals seemed so far-fetched, but we just kept taking action, and within a short few years we were able to see the result of our work.

Be kind to others, but most importantly be kind to yourself. The time is now. Focus on your dreams, and you'll figure it out along the way despite how far-fetched your dreams may seem. Kaitlyn, Amy, and Kolton, just do it . . . because you deserve it and you can!

Love always,
Mom and Dave/Dad

CONTENTS

Acknowledgments..vii

Introduction 1

Chapter 1 Excuses Are the Lies We Tell Ourselves 9

Chapter 2 Bring Home the Cash Cows 17

Chapter 3 Win-Win Negotiations 27

Chapter 4 Get Rich by Using Debt 35

Chapter 5 Tenants: The 97 Percent Principle 41

Chapter 6 Sh*t Happens . . . Deal with It!..................... 47

Chapter 7 If They Don't Know You, It's Your Fault 55

Chapter 8 Even the King of the Jungle
Can't Do It Alone 63

Chapter 9 The Perfect Time Is Now.............................. 71

About the Authors 79

We'll Put Your Money To Work For You! 82

Mentoring Programs 83

ACKNOWLEDGMENTS

We would like to give thanks to our family who love us unconditionally.

Melanie would like to thank her mom, Mariette Fleury, who is a one-of-a-kind woman. She taught me not to worry about other people's opinions. When I happened to do so, she would quickly stop me in my tracks and tell me "who cares" and to do what makes me happy. Most importantly, Mom gave me the gift of unconditional love. Thanks Dad, JC Fleury, whom I have always been able to count on whenever I needed help. It's no doubt that my sales and business skills were taken directly from you. Thank you both for all your love and support.

I'm also very grateful for my grandparents, Florida and Eugene Lafond, who loved and spoiled me. One of my last and favorite moments with Grand-maman was on my wedding day, when unexpectedly, in front of everyone, at ninety years old, she started singing "Un

Coin du Ciel." Her kindness and free spirit will be forever cherished.

Thank you to my best friend and husband, Dave Dupuis, who has always been there for me and helped me believe that together we can realize all of our dreams. I'm fortunate to spend my days laughing and doing what I love with you.

Dave would like to thank his mom, Lise Dupuis. You always put my needs and wants in front of your own. Your selfless acts of caring and giving inspired me to do the same and pass that on to the kids. Thank you also to my late dad, Michel Dupuis, who taught me many good lessons. Among them, he showed me the value of laughter and of doing what I love doing despite what others may think. I hope to come even close to the legacy he left! Thank you to my baby sister, Natalie Dupuis, whom I love so much, and her soon-to-be husband, Mat Blanchfield. Pa would be so proud of you.

Thank you to my aunts Nancy Sauvé and Crista Bezel. You two were like second moms to me, and I could always turn to you for sound advice and reasoning. Thank you to my mémère Gisele Sauvé, who has taught me that age is truly just a number. Your energy, resilience, and love for life are admirable, and I hope to follow in your footsteps.

I want to give a special thank you to my wife, Melanie Dupuis. Thank you for being my rock, my best friend, and the best wife I could have ever dreamed of. I'm extremely lucky to have also found the best business partner I could ask for in the same person I love and share my life with.

Thank you to everyone involved with making deals happen, including our real estate agent, lawyer's office, accountant, private lenders, and insurance brokers.

Thank you to all of our tenants for giving us the opportunity to find and rent you a home, and for being caring and respectful. You certainly showed us that "tenant horror stories" are few and far between.

Thank you to our amazing Dupuis Properties team, who are committed to meeting deadlines, finding solutions, and producing quality work. We couldn't do this without you.

Thank you to our friends who believe in us, encourage us, and bring much joy and laughter in our world.

Finally, thank you to Helen Chang, Jenny Shipley, and the Author Bridge Media team for your editorial and publishing services.

INTRODUCTION

Shackled

You are thinking about getting started in real estate investing.

You may be stuck working in an unfulfilling job or one that doesn't have much opportunity for expansion. You're working for a paycheck. You have to put in forty hours a week to get your predetermined pay. If you want more money, you have to work overtime, sell more on commission, or get a second job. You want to dream big . . . but you don't want to work eighty hours a week to support those dreams. How are you supposed to do this for the next forty years?

On the flip side, your forty-hour-a-week job that you are stuck in for the foreseeable future offers some security. It's a guaranteed paycheck.

Security, however, is the opposite of freedom. It's something that locks you in. It's shackles.

And we want to show you how you can walk away from the job that holds you captive and finally find financial freedom.

Freedom Awaits

Real estate investing is a proven path to wealth and freedom.

When you work nine to five, you're working to make someone else rich. When you invest in your own real estate education and portfolio, you're working to make yourself rich. That allows you the freedom to pursue your dreams and long-term goals.

The beauty of real estate investing is that there's no limit to how much money you can make. When done correctly, it can be one of the most lucrative investments that you can make—even earning you money while you sleep. This opens up more opportunities for yourself, your family, and future generations. It is your responsibility to create that freedom for yourself and those you love.

We're here to tell you the truth about real estate investing—the good, the bad, and the ugly—so that you can get started on your journey to wealth and freedom with a clear picture of what to expect. That being said, even when it's ugly, it's still so good!

Back to the Beginning

Let's look at how we got started in real estate investing.

Dave's Story: My Ticket to Success

In high school, one of my friends lent me a book about real estate investing. I loved the whole concept of providing a home to someone while simultaneously making money. I loved real estate and noticed those who became successful because of it. I wanted to be "that guy," and I had a gut feeling that it would be my ticket to success.

I was just waiting for the perfect time to get started.

And that's where I was—working my full-time job, eventually buying a single-family house to rent out—when I met Melanie. She already had a couple of rentals at the time, so she helped me jump in with both feet. I finally stopped making up excuses and used her experience to get me through that initial learning curve.

Melanie's Story: Landlord Without Limits

When I went to college, I moved from apartment to apartment: some nice, some okay, and some questionable. One time, I moved into a place with a nonworking fridge and faulty plumbing (hot showers were always a miracle). I remember thinking that if I were a landlord, I would have much higher standards than this.

Years after graduating, I bought my first property, and then I bought a second. And then I had an epiphany: there's no limit to how many properties I could acquire and no cap on how much money I could make.

Years passed by, and then I met Dave. I saw his drive and passion for real estate investing, and I was confident that we would do this together . . . in a huge way!

Better Together

After three years investing together, we experienced explosive growth. We finally learned the things we needed to learn, and we were able to buy twelve properties in one year.

As of the end of 2018, we own twenty-two buildings with a total of eighty-seven units.

This is not us bragging. We are sharing this for you to realize how you can significantly change your financial situation in a matter of a few years. You have to start somewhere—and you have to get started!

What We Wish We'd Known

We wrote this book because we wish we'd had a guide like this one.

We remember feeling scared, making excuses, and not being sure our goals were even attainable. In fact, that's how we felt just a couple of years ago. If we'd known from the start what we know now, we would have avoided some costly mistakes.

The real estate investing world is not always going to be perfect. And you're still going to make some mistakes; we all do. But we're going to show you our secrets, things you can do to make better decisions the first time, so you can learn from our mistakes and save yourself tons of time and money—and grow even faster than we have! This book is going to save you one or two—maybe even three—years of taking baby steps and help you fast-forward straight to your tremendous growth. We can't remove the learning curve completely, but we can help smooth out some of the bumps.

This is not the only way to be successful in real estate, but this is our story. This is how we did it—and how we're still doing it. Take the advice and adjust it to suit your own lifestyle, and you'll be able to achieve your goals based on your own needs.

This book is short on purpose. We want you to actually be able to read it—all in one sitting, if possible. As you read, highlight or write down whatever sticks out to you, whatever triggers a reaction—good or bad. Take those as wake-up calls or personal challenges. You may not like everything we say, but this is a no-B.S. book. Maybe that's a sign that we're the kick in the butt you need. We want to get you out of your comfort zone and make you realize it's time to get started.

Just get started. Everything else will come.

Your Path Starts Here

It's now your time to jump on this opportunity. It's time to change things up.

Stop doing what you have been doing. You aren't fully happy or fulfilled, which is why you're reading this book now. So open your mind to a different way of looking at things. Let go of the fear, and take the plunge. Challenge yourself to make this a success. Anything less should be unacceptable.

Because you *can* do this! You just need to believe in yourself. Believe that you can do it, and believe that you're no longer alone, because we're here to guide you through it.

Once you turn this page, you have made a commitment to yourself. You are declaring, "I'm ready to do this! I'm ready for success . . . I'm ready for financial freedom!"

Chapter 1

EXCUSES ARE THE LIES WE TELL OURSELVES

Off the Fence

Is your bum getting numb? Been sitting on the fence about real estate investing for too long? Are you tired of watching yet another opportunity sail away?

Hop off the fence and jump feet first into real estate investing!

Once you create enough cash flow from your real estate portfolio, you will no longer have to stress about or care when the next payday is. Thanks to your healthy bank account, those worries will disappear. You can finally sail into your sunset of wealth and freedom.

But we're not going to lie: it's not all sunshine and butterflies. (No B.S., remember?)

You've heard some success stories. You've also heard all the reasons why you shouldn't invest in real estate. You want to make more money, but you don't want to deal with clogged toilets, middle-of-the-night phone calls, and late rent payments. You're scared to get started, scared of taking a big risk, and scared of the unknown.

And that's why you're reading this book.

To get the *real* story. To learn real lessons from real people. And to discover the secret of how real estate investing can take you from "What if?" to "Why not?"

Benefits of Real Estate Investing

But why do we love real estate investing so much? (No, it's not all overflowing toilets and nightmare tenants . . . quite the opposite!)

The financial perk is the monthly cash flow. We love to see money coming in every month. And the best part is that our equity builds every month as tenants pay down our mortgages.

Although we do have some single-family dwellings and commercial buildings, we prefer to have multi-family residential income because everyone will always need a place to call home. And the more units you have, the more insulation you have against issues that come with non-payment of rent. Some of the general principles of investing in real estate apply across the board, no matter how you're investing. But the scope of this book is going to focus on multi-family homes.

Real estate investing has proven over time to be the best investment you can make. As you continue to acquire more properties, you can break through the shackles of "security" from your job and move toward financial freedom.

But the biggest benefit of investing in real estate is that once you have enough cash cows, you can replace your current income, become your own boss, and be completely in charge of your own time. It's total freedom!

That's huge for us. We get to watch our kids hop on the bus in the morning. We're home when they return from school. And we can join them on school field trips without feeling guilty for taking time off work. We get to have this precious time with them that we will never get back.

"I Don't Have Enough Time" and Other B.S. Excuses

So why haven't you started investing in real estate yet?

We have heard a *lot* of excuses about why other people haven't started investing in real estate, and they are all bullsh*t.

Here are a few of the most common excuses we hear—and what you can do if you have made any of these excuses yourself.

I don't have enough time. We all have the same twenty-four hours in a day. How can you maximize those hours to add value in your life? Can you give up some TV shows, get up earlier, or limit your social media time? You can find balance and still focus on your goals.

Just the fact that you are reading this book means that you have time to take the first step. Don't waste that momentum!

I don't have enough money. We understand. We didn't have enough money when we first got started, either. So Dave worked every extra shift he could, Melanie started teaching online college courses, and we both cut back on luxuries. We did what most people wouldn't do, for a short amount of time, so that in the long term we could have the life that most people won't be able to have.

Do you have cable? Cut that. Two birds, one stone. You save money and create extra time by getting rid of a distraction.

I'm afraid I'll lose it all. One of the excuses we hear most often is the risk of losing money. It's always, "I know somebody who had a lot of real estate, but everything went to hell, and they lost it all."

Restaurants go belly-up all the time. Retail stores fail. People lose money in the stock market every day. Real estate investing is no different from anything else. If you don't do your homework, you're vulnerable. If you do, real estate is the most solid investment, because everybody needs a home.

We'll show you how to minimize your risk of losing money by making educated, calculated decisions. Knowing what to do and what not to do can help take away your fear.

If you want to take yourself to the next level, you need to stop making excuses and take some educated risks. As Mark Zuckerberg says, "The biggest risk is not taking a risk."

The Path to Financial Freedom

You are about to embark on the path to financial freedom. From finding a deal to creating your ultimate vision, you will find eight steps on the path ahead, each one addressed in a separate chapter:

Bring Home the Cash Cows. Learning how to find cash cows, or really great deals, will help you reduce your risk and increase your revenue. In this chapter, we'll teach you how to find the properties that will bring you success in real estate investing.

Win-Win Negotiations. Once you find the right cash-flowing property, the next step is to negotiate the purchase. Our win-win formula makes sure that you and the seller both walk away happy.

Get Rich by Using Debt. Erase what you know about money, because you're going to learn a whole new way of looking at it. We will show you that debt is one of the most powerful tools you can use.

Tenants: The 97 Percent Principle. We came up with this figure based on our experience: the majority of our tenants are awesome, but some of them are not. We're going to show you how to minimize your risks so that 97 percent of your tenants are awesome too.

Sh*t Happens . . . Deal with It! It's as simple as that. You'll learn how to deal with some of the issues that all landlords experience, so you can stop complaining, implement a solution, and move on to finding your next big deal.

If They Don't Know You, It's Your Fault. If people don't know you, you will have a much harder time finding cash cows, lenders, and tenants. We'll show you how to use innovative marketing, social media, and networking to make sure people know your name.

Even the King of the Jungle Can't Do It Alone. If you want to take your success in real estate investing to the next level, you won't be able to do it alone. We'll show you how to build an elite team of people who can help you make more money.

The Perfect Time Is Now. Everything you are about to learn comes together in this final chapter. Together, we will create your ultimate vision for your real estate investing career.

Before we start down this path, take out a piece of paper and write down your purpose. Why do you want to invest in real estate?

Is it to get rich? Is it to leave more money for your kids? Do you need to fund your retirement or want to leave your job?

Now look at it again. If your reason is materialistic, write another one, because it can't all be about the toys money can buy. So what is it *really* about for you? Find your real purpose, because nice things alone aren't going to be enough to get you through the hard times.

Post that piece of paper where you will see it every day.

With that purpose in hand, it's time to walk the rest of the path to financial freedom. There's no turning back now, just turning the next page. Chapter 2 will show you how to find cash cows.

Chapter 2

Bring Home the Cash Cows

The Sky's the Limit

If you had told us when we were first starting out that we would end up owning twenty-two properties, and buying twelve of them in one year, we would have thought you were crazy.

But in 2017, we acquired twelve investment properties in twelve months.

It all began making sense for us when we realized that one of our properties paid us per month the same amount that Mel made every two weeks at her full-time job. So we knew that if we got two buildings like that, it would equal her whole salary—more than $80,000 a year.

And if we had twelve of them, well . . . the sky's the limit!

Cash Cows

How were we able to buy twelve properties in twelve months? We invested in cash cows!

A cash cow is any investment property that makes a substantial cash flow per month. Basically, once you receive all rent and pay all expenses, the amount left over is your monthly cash flow. Whether substantial cash flow means $500 or $5,000 at this point in your investing career, if you want to find copious success, you have to find cash cows.

Cash-cow buildings allow you to grow much more quickly. If the properties you find don't cash flow very well, you'll find real estate investing very difficult. With cash cows, however, you'll have flexibility with your portfolio and opportunity for rapid growth. That means you're on track to finding financial freedom for you and your family.

To evaluate whether a deal may be a cash cow, you have to know your market, know your numbers, and know the potential.

Know Your Market

In order to find cash cows, you have to know what one looks like when you see it. And that means you have to know your market.

What does a duplex go for in your area? What is the average rent of a one- or two-bedroom apartment? What is the average per-door market sale price? In our market, the per-door (or per-unit) average is $100,000. So if someone wants to sell us a triplex for $450,000, we already know that it won't meet our cash-cow standards, and we don't waste our time exploring it.

We can't teach you your market, because each market is unique and always changing. The only way for you to learn it is to do your research and look at it daily.

So if you are starting off, go see some properties. In fact, go see a *lot* of properties. Have you been to an open house yet? Search on Kijiji or Craigslist to see what's available. If you want to invest in a different area, learn that market.

This is to be done only when you are initially learning about your market. Once you understand your market, don't waste your time on this any longer, but keep your finger on the pulse.

Know Your Numbers

Once you know your market, you have to make sure the numbers work for the potential investment properties you find.

The basic, very quick and dirty rule of thumb to get a fast feel for whether a property makes sense in terms of cash flow is to calculate 1 percent of the asking price. If the total gross monthly income is 1 percent or more of the asking price, it's worth moving forward. If, however, the gross income falls below 0.7 percent of the asking price, then you don't want to waste your time.

To help with your cash flow analysis, you will want to look at all incomes and all expenses for that building.

Income means all the rents, parking, coin-operated laundry, solar panels, and anything else that brings money into the property. This is where you can also guesstimate if there's potential for growth—hence why knowing your market is crucial. The expenses are everything that has to be paid, no matter who owns it. Remember, as you calculate the mortgage, that loan terms, rates, and down-payment amounts vary from one person to another.

Don't forget about other expenses such as gas,

hydro, water, insurance, property taxes, property maintenance, property management, snow removal, yard maintenance, and potential vacancy. We like to leave 5 percent for vacancy (even though our numbers are much lower) and 5–10 percent for maintenance and management costs. We may as well do a worst-case scenario, because the underwriters at the financial institution are going to calculate it that way before financing the deal.

When the total from all income leaves you a substantial profit after all expenses are taken into consideration, you know that your cash cow has come home.

For example, a few years ago, we bought a bank-repossessed, run-down duplex with two two-bedroom units for $119,000. It was previously a drug house and in desperate need of cosmetic work. We spent $20,000 in renovations that were completed within a month of acquisition. The building was afterwards appraised at $225,000. After all costs, including renovations and closing, we had more than $86,000 in active appreciation. We refinanced, bought more cash cows, and the building now gives us a cash flow of $1,250 net a month.

When is the last time your other investments paid

you more than $85,000 *tax-free* in less than a year? Now that's sexy!

Know the Potential

After you have looked at a lot of deals and made sure the numbers make sense, you want to look at underperforming properties as well.

These are properties where the tenants are not paying fair market value rent. If they are underperforming, you have the potential to increase the rent whenever you have an old tenant move out and a new one move in.

A building may be underperforming for many reasons. Maybe it's unattractive, maybe the previous landlord had great tenants and didn't want to increase their rent over the years, or maybe the expenses are too high.

We bought an unattractive, underperforming building that had tons of potential. We had to look past the holes in the walls, green shag carpet, pet-urine smell, and pink bathroom. But we weren't scared away; we were excited. The rents were well below fair market price, but, most importantly, the property was still cash flowing from day one, so we knew this was going to be a cash cow.

We painted the outside and put on a new roof, and now it looks like an entirely new building. As tenants moved out, we did some minor renovations and, as a result, raised the rent more than $600 per unit. This building made money from day one, but now our yearly cash flow has almost tripled!

Having a portfolio of cash cows gives you the flexibility to purchase a building that is underperforming but has the potential for huge upside. The numbers may not currently make sense to the financial institution, but lenders look at your entire portfolio. When you have other cash cows, they can support this building until it becomes a cash cow as well.

This tactic has been very lucrative for us, because we look at countless deals to find the diamonds in the rough. When we find them, we transform them into cash cows and then refinance or sell them at a much higher value. This enables us to take that money and keep buying more properties.

Ka-¢hing!

Not all the deals we find turn into the cash cows we actually acquire. Here are our tried and true steps that we use to help narrow it down:

1. Ensure that the property is located in a city and neighborhood you want to invest in.
2. Make sure the numbers make sense or that the property is an underperforming building. It should make enough money to cover all your expenses and still have positive cash flow from day one.
3. Look at pictures. At a quick glance, is the place in good condition? Does it need a lot of work? We highly suggest not judging a book by its cover. We bought that ugly underperforming building even though it stuck out like a sore thumb. Once we did the cash flow analysis and saw that the property made money *and* had through-the-roof potential, we were willing to accept the work necessary to bring it up to our cash-cow standards.

For every fifty potential properties in our area, the numbers may make sense for only ten. Once we do our more in-depth cash flow analysis, we probably look at only two or three of those buildings—and ultimately, we may buy only one or two out of the original fifty. But we know that when we do, they are going to keep making us money for years to come.

Chapter 2: Bring Home the Cash Cows

Once you find that cash cow for yourself, you're going to want it now! And you should want to jump through any hoops to get it. But how can you make that process go more smoothly and be satisfying for you *and* the seller? Turn the page to find out about win-win negotiations in chapter 3.

Chapter 3

WIN-WIN NEGOTIATIONS

The Right Time

When we first started real estate investing together, we fell in love with a seven-unit building. We really wanted it.

But the time wasn't right.

The seller hadn't done necessary repairs, the bank wouldn't approve it, and the numbers didn't make sense. We had to walk away.

A couple of years later, however, Dave drove by the property and saw the owner outside. He pulled over, introduced himself, and asked, "Would you be interested in making a deal?"

This time was the right time. The seller's situation

had changed, and he was motivated to sell. He'd done the upgrades, and now the numbers made sense.

In the first year of owning that building, we doubled the cash flow and increased its value by $200,000!

Everybody Wins

When we bought that building, the seller got motivated buyers, which resulted in an easy sale, and we got a great investment. We call that a win-win . . . and that's one of our biggest secrets.

Win-win negotiations mean that both sides walk away happy. You get more or less what you want out of the deal, and the sellers get more or less what they want as well.

That's important, because when sellers feel good, they're going to talk positively about the transaction. Also, if they have more buildings to sell or—even more likely—if they know someone who wants to sell a building, they will keep you in mind.

If you are focusing only on winning, then the seller automatically becomes the loser. Nobody likes to lose. Yes, you might save a few thousand dollars, but you don't want to be known as the buyer who tries to lowball every deal. That news will travel quickly, and that's never what an investor wants. You want sellers to *want* to contact you when they are ready to sell their buildings.

This chapter will show you how to win on your next deal by putting in an offer, negotiating fairly, and knowing when to walk away.

Don't Be Afraid to Make an Offer

We're going to tell you something that's different from what most other people will say: don't be afraid to make offers and then figure it out later.

When we find a deal, we do the numbers quickly. We look at the property on Google Earth, talk to the realtors if they've walked through the building before, and look at pictures. Then, if it seems to make sense, we put in an offer. We don't want to miss out on the building, so as soon as the numbers work and we like the property, we just do it.

Don't be afraid to put in offers; they're free! With the right conditions in your offer, you will be able to walk away from the offer if necessary. Once you get that deal under contract, time is on your side. *This* is when you have time to walk through the building if you haven't already done so and get an inspection to make an educated decision.

Better this way than doing all your homework first, then finding out that someone else pulled the trigger before you.

Negotiate to Win-Win

Once you find a cash cow, the numbers make sense, and you've put in an offer, then you want to figure out a deal that benefits you and the seller.

A lot of people will look at a building, see an asking price of $200,000, and think, "I want it for $175,000, because I want to get a deal."

We've made that mistake before, so now we don't focus on trying to get the lowest price possible. We used to be so focused on trying to save $10,000, $15,000, or $20,000 that we didn't look at the bigger picture. We would have made back that money in monthly cash flow within a year (not to mention appreciation and mortgage recapture) if we hadn't been so focused on the purchase price.

Yes, you want to pay a good price. But you don't want to insult the seller in the process. You're not just buying a house, here; you're buying into your own reputation as an investor. And your reputation matters!

The other part of the bigger picture is asking yourself whether you're going to be okay losing this cash-flowing building over a mere $5,000 or $10,000. If that price difference makes or breaks the deal, it clearly wasn't a cash cow in the first place.

Finally, the last rule of negotiating is to find out what the seller's motivation is. Let the seller talk first, ask your questions—and then listen to discover what he or she wants. Then you can tap into that and really structure the deal around it. If you aren't dealing directly with the seller, you must ensure that your realtor is on the same page.

For example, if the seller doesn't want to negotiate on the full asking price, that's okay. If the building cash flows, you can give the seller his or her full asking price. But maybe you ask for an updated fire retrofit, new shingles, or the outside to be painted. If sellers are motivated by a quick closing, or by closing at a specific time for capital gains or tax purposes, then you give them whatever closing day they want in exchange for the conditions you want.

When you give the seller what he or she wants, and

you get what you want—a cash-flowing property—you both win.

Know When to Walk Away

At some point in some deals, you may just have to walk away. Here are a few examples of when that should happen:

- You receive quotes, and you would have to spend significantly more than predicted on renovations.
- You have an inspection done, and you find issues that are a deal breaker for you, such as foundation, mold, knob and tube, etc.
- The financial institution is not willing to finance the building because it's currently underperforming.
- The financing terms received are not what you had expected (higher interest rate, lower loan-to-value, etc.).
- The seller won't give you anything that you want in your conditions, especially with big items such as environmental assessments and

fire retrofit. You don't want to be in a win-lose situation!

Any time you try to determine the risk but you don't have all the information for an educated calculation, we recommend walking away. That will leave you more time for the deals that *do* make sense for you.

Take a Moment to Reflect

After every deal—whether you close on it or end up walking away—take a moment to reflect.

Think about what went well and what didn't go well—or what could go better next time. And if you closed the deal, take a moment to celebrate. Enjoy the win. You are on your way to being the owner of a cash-flowing investment property—and that's exciting!

Feel that excitement, learn from what you've done well—and then keep doing it. You're only going to get better and better with every deal you do.

You have already taken huge steps on the path to financial freedom. But the next step is finding the funding for your investment, and you don't want that to be your stumbling block. Chapter 4 will help the process go smoothly.

Chapter 4

GET RICH BY USING DEBT

No Pain, No Gain

When we first met, Mel had just purchased a brand-new vehicle.

However, we really wanted to get into real estate investing, so we needed to lower our expenses and better our debt-recovery ratios. Then the lenders would have no choice but to approve our rental property purchases!

So she got rid of her beautiful new SUV, and we went down to one vehicle. We drove around in an embarrassing, beat-up, rusty old van for years. Everybody made fun of it, because not only was it falling apart, but it also made loud noises. Frankly, it sucked.

But we were willing to experience some short-term pain for long-term gain.

We had to check our pride and set it aside. While people laughed at us, we knew that we were doing what we needed to do. We lowered our expenses, invested, and built our portfolio.

Now, only a few years later, we have the last laugh, because we've both been able to buy nice vehicles that we've always wanted with the cash flow from our properties.

Debt-Free Is *Not* for Me

When we were younger, we were taught that debt was bad, and being mortgage-free was something to strive for.

This is an outdated and non-investor way of thinking. If given the choice between being mortgage-free and having a big fat mortgage, we choose the latter every day. Let us explain why this is one of our secrets.

Two types of debt exist: bad debt and good debt.

Bad debt is debt spent on things that don't generate revenue—trips, new vehicles, large TVs . . . basically, most consumer goods. Good debt is the type that pays for itself and also makes you a profit. An example is a mortgage on a house—if used properly. That means if you refinance your mortgage, take the equity out of your house, and lend it at a higher interest rate, that debt can be considered good debt.

Debt can be a powerful tool if used correctly—and if used together with other tools in your toolbox for the greatest success.

In this chapter, we are going to talk about short-term sacrifices for long-term gain, and how to use debt—other people's money—to get rich.

Do What You Don't Want to Do Now, so You Can Do Whatever You Want Later

Choose to do the things you don't want to do now, so you can choose to do whatever you want later.

We made short-term sacrifices. We got rid of Melanie's new SUV, didn't buy the latest iPhone, and held off on buying new furniture and a big home. In order to get to the next level, it may be helpful—perhaps even necessary—for you also to be frugal temporarily and reduce your expenses.

But if you don't have thick enough skin to do something different and make the sacrifices now, then you may not be cut out to be a real estate investor.

You have to evaluate yourself. Not everybody is made to invest in real estate, and that's okay. But if you think you can make those choices and give yourself the reality check, then this is absolutely for you.

Because don't get us wrong—we wanted all the new, shiny, fun things. We just wanted wealth and freedom more.

Use Other People's Money to Get Rich

One form of good debt is using Other People's Money, or OPM, to purchase your investment property—again, as long as this tool is used properly.

Imagine a partnership that allows you to purchase an investment property and you only have to come up with the down payment. You can use your partner's money to pay the rest. And this partner is silent: you're not getting any feedback or pushback. Finally, they let you keep the monthly cash flow, any tax write-offs, and all the equity. When you sell the property, you get to keep the profit. Sounds pretty good, doesn't it?

If you haven't guessed already, the partner is the bank, the private lender, or the mortgage broker—the "other people" whose money you can use to get rich in real estate investing.

But you always want to leverage debt to your advantage by using it wisely. Don't refinance your mortgage (which is OPM) and go on a trip or buy a new vehicle, because that doesn't make you any money. It costs money. Instead, put that money toward a down payment and buy another property. Refinance it or sell it at a higher value. Then repay the OPM and take the profit to fund your next cash cow. Once you have enough properties, the income from those properties can buy you your new truck, sports car, or dream home.

You always need to ensure you have an exit strategy to pay back the OPM.

If it can't be done with the property you're interested in, walk away! Many real estate investors fail because they don't have a plan A, B, *and* C to pay back their lenders. Paying back the OPM is as important as—if not more important than—getting the money to buy that building in the first place. We are so committed to paying our OPM that we would sell our primary residence before ever losing the golden goose. We can always buy another house, but we can never buy back broken trust and reputation.

All this being said, if you have a secured exit strategy and you are confident in your cash cow, then you can purchase the building with no money down by using 100 percent OPM!

A Better Way

If you want to own eighty-seven units like we do, you won't be able to use your own money for the down payment—unless you have very deep pockets. Even Apple, one of the richest companies in the world, uses debt and OPM. Don't you think if being debt-free was better, Apple would do that instead?

If you're reading this and thinking, "I really don't have the time to become a real estate investor," or "I don't want to be this hands-on; I just want to make money," or even, "I have investment money, and I just want to earn monthly interest," then reach out to us. We're always looking to do business with private lenders. Call us at (705) 491-1058 or email us at realestateinvesting@dupuisproperties.com, and we'll put your money to work 24/7—and you can cash flow from *our* cash cows! It's a win-win partnership.

Now that you have your cash cow and know how you're going to pay for it, it's time to look at where your income begins: rent, and the tenants who pay it. Chapter 5 will show you how to find the best tenants to fill your cash-flowing properties.

Chapter 5

TENANTS: THE 97 PERCENT PRINCIPLE

Livin' in Love

As landlords, we provide homes for people to live in. And those buildings are home to some pretty happy moments!

In fact, two of our tenants met when they moved in across the hall from one another. After a few months, they started dating and became a couple. When they eventually gave us the great news that they were ready to move in together, they moved into the bigger of the two units and have since had their first child together.

We love to promote the good stories about real estate investing. Being a landlord is awesome!

Just a Few Bad Apples

In our experience, most tenants are awesome. In fact, we've come up with our own principle. From all the tenants we've had, 97 percent of them, on average, are great, respectful tenants.

The other 3 percent? Well, they're . . . not so good. And having bad tenants can put you and your investment at risk of property damage, unpaid rent, and losing good tenants who currently live in that property. Good tenants, however, treat your house like their home. And that's the 97 percent you'll be happy to have living in your buildings—and paying rent—for as long as possible.

If you do all the things we'll talk about in this chapter, you'll find that principle to be true for you too!

In this chapter, we are going to look at how to find those great tenants and how to keep them.

How to Find Awesome Tenants

Even if the building is full when you buy it, you will inevitably receive a notice to move out at some point. And that means that you will have to find new tenants.

Chapter 5: Tenants: The 97 Percent Principle 43

So why shouldn't you just take the first person who offers you cash? Because you want the best tenants possible! That means doing your due diligence, just like you do for every other step of investing in real estate. And we have a process for that.

First, as soon as we have a unit available, we post it on our website, social media, and Kijiji or Craigslist. You want as much exposure as possible to get a big pool of potential tenants to choose from. Adding pictures of the clean and tidy property is a must!

After that, we have an initial phone interview where we ensure that the potential tenant has all the details. We reiterate price, location, number of bedrooms, and move-in date to make sure that it meets the potential tenant's criteria. We also ask if the potential tenant has first and last month's rent.

If we're on the same page, we set up a viewing.

A face-to-face meeting is a great way to get to know the potential tenant. Ask lots of questions, and spend most of the time listening. If you find red flags, think twice before choosing these people as your new renters. These are the people who will live in your investment. They will pay the rent, which, in turn, pays the mortgage. So it's important to always trust your gut. Every time we have ignored that and gone for the quick rent, we've kicked ourselves afterwards. It's just not worth it.

If no red flags go up when you show the place, you have almost filled that vacancy. Just a few more steps remain.

Google the potential tenants' names, and take a look at their social media accounts to see if you find any red flags. Call current and past landlords. We are shocked that most landlords do not do this! It takes only a few minutes and can avoid a nightmare tenant. Ask the landlord questions: How are the tenants on rent? How clean are they? How are they with other tenants? Would you rent to this person again? You may also choose to do a credit check.

If you are happy with the feedback and no red flags have popped up, proceed with collecting a copy of the potential tenants' identification, the last month's rent, and their proof of income. This is when you can provide them with a copy of the lease to complete and sign.

If you follow all of our steps, you are going to eliminate most of your potential problem tenants. As long as you're doing everything legally and legitimately, you can rest easy at night.

How to Keep Your Awesome Tenants

The most important part of finding good tenants is keeping them!

We treat all our tenants with understanding and respect—just like we expect them to treat us and our properties.

We don't believe in locking our tenants into contracts. If this isn't the right place for them, we don't want to force them to stay. And if they have to move, we want to support them. In fact, we give the tenants who pay rent on time and are clean and respectful "VIP Tenant" privilege. This is a special incentive that gives great tenants first priority in renting any of our other properties that become available.

We'll also do little things to beautify the place. If we're at the property, we'll clean up trash or pick up cigarette butts. This shows the tenants that we care—and then they care more too.

These things may seem little, and they don't take much time, money, or effort, but they make a huge difference. They show you care about the property, which means your awesome tenants are much more likely to take care of the property and let you know if anything else needs your attention—before it becomes a humongous problem.

Dave's Story: My Biggest Fear

When we started out, one of my biggest fears was how to find tenants. This held me back for a long time, because I had built this barrier up so much in my mind: How do I find people? How do I qualify them? I was completely overwhelmed and intimidated by all these unknowns.

For a while, that fear crippled me. It kept me from the things I wanted—real estate, equity, and cash flow.

But then I met Mel, and she squashed those fears by helping me realize I was making excuses. "It's not earth-shattering," she told me. "People all over the world do this every day. You just put a process in place and then follow it."

I'm so glad she cleared that big mental roadblock for me, so we can have the success—and financial freedom—that we now enjoy.

We hope that puts your mind at ease too. We know you've been waiting for the tenant nightmare stories—and we do have some to share. You'll have to turn to chapter 6 to read what to do when sh*t happens.

Chapter 6

SH*T HAPPENS ... DEAL WITH IT!

Horror Stories

We've all heard the general, small horror stories of being a landlord: units left dirty, finding holes in the walls, late rent payment. These are frustrations, sure. But hell tenants? Not really.

We have had some hell tenants and some landlord horror stories too.

First, there was the tenant who worked for the "federal government" and, the second he moved in, stopped paying rent and expected to live there rent-free. We had to endure the long process of going through the tenant board. Once we had a judgment, then we had to go through the court system to garnish his wages through his employer. We had to spend Dave's entire birthday in court just to get back the thousands of dollars we were owed.

Then there was the tenant we inherited when we purchased a building and who was an issue from the day we met him. He rewired the electricity (including the smoke detectors!), smoked inside the nonsmoking building, got intoxicated and peed off his balcony, and constantly disturbed other tenants. In fact, we lost numerous amazing tenants because of him.

Or how about the tenant we had to evict? He left months' worth of garbage and dirty dishes, damaged the property, and kept showing up screaming until the police had to come and physically remove him . . . multiple times.

These are some of our horror stories. But the reason they stand out is because they are the exceptions to the rule. And did we let these few bad experiences get us down?

Absolutely not!

Sh*t Happens

For us, having wealth and freedom is worth the hassle of the few horror stories we have experienced. Despite the 3 percent we've had to deal with, we would do it all over again.

Is it worth it to you? Are you willing to deal with these less-than-ideal situations once in a while, if it means that you can make as much money as you want? (Keep in mind, once you have enough cash flow, you can hire someone to deal with these situations for you!) If you want that for yourself—if you want cash flow and all the awesome benefits of investing in real estate—sh*t is going to happen to you too.

When we first started, we worried a lot, wondering, "What if sh*t happens?" The no-B.S. reality is that it's not "what if." It's "*when*." And *when* sh*t happens, you will need to deal with it.

Every time sh*t happens, that's an opportunity for you to take action, implement or improve your policies, and then learn from it so it doesn't happen again.

Mel loves a motivational quote that says, "The size of your problems is nothing compared with your ability to solve them. Don't overestimate your problems and underestimate yourself."

In this chapter, you're going to learn how to just deal with it and how to prevent some sh*t from happening in the first place.

Deal with It!

When sh*t happens, don't build it up into a huge mountain to overcome. Don't waste time whining and complaining. Instead, use that time to take action and find solutions.

Don't take it personally; just turn to your process and . . . deal with it. Because you *can*. (We promise!) You just need to realize that everything is a process. Just deal with it, step by step, and you'll get through it.

If it's the second of the month, and you haven't received rent yet from one of your tenants, what do you do? Sh*t happens . . . deal with it!

But how do I deal with it?

Well, in this example, you would provide the tenant with a form for nonpayment of rent.

I don't know what that is.

Well, look online for who the governing body is for landlords and tenants in your province or state. Then, find the necessary form for nonpayment of rent. All you have to do is print it, fill it out, and put it in their mailbox. And boom, away you go—just dealt with it!

That's the mindset you need to have in order to be successful in real estate investing. Don't be problem-oriented. Be problem-solving.

What Can I Do to Prevent Sh*t in the First Place?

Once you've dealt with an issue and fixed the problem, ask yourself, "How can I prevent this from happening again? How can I prevent *other* sh*t like it from happening?"

We've talked about reducing your risk in real estate investing. Well, this is how you reduce the chances of sh*t happening as a landlord.

The biggest thing you can do is take the thinking out of it. Make everything automatic, because everyone forgets something sometimes. Creating checklists means that you don't have to try to remember everything.

Our team members—meaning us as well—have missed things when we turn over apartments. So now we've created a spreadsheet that details every single thing that needs to be done after one tenant moves out and before the next tenant can move in. Does every window have a screen? Can all the doors lock? Has the refrigerator been cleaned? Our staff goes down the list and checks everything off, and we know it's all been done.

The other side of prevention is preventive work, which will save you time and money in the long run.

Don't just wait for things to happen. Be proactive. Check with your tenants to make sure their apartment is fine, that they're not waiting to tell you about something until it becomes a big issue. Have the roof checked, and repair it *before* it starts to leak.

And if something is broken, just fix it—and fix it right. Putting it off or being cheap will only create bigger problems. Communicate that to your tenants. That way they'll know you're doing walk-throughs and regular fire checks to make sure everything is in good working order and stays that way.

Growth

Real estate investing is like planting a tree.

It's very time-consuming at the start. You have to prep the soil, plant the tree, and water it. You have to put in the effort. This is where most of the sh*t happens—before you implement your processes and policies—but you can use that as fertilizer.

Then things start happening. The tree grows some roots, and it doesn't need you as much anymore. Once in a while you give it some TLC, but for the most part your real estate portfolio becomes a self-sustained, well-oiled machine.

The tree flowers and bears fruit, but it doesn't happen overnight, just like your real estate investment is not a get-rich-overnight scheme.

Instead, it's a plan so that you can make money 24/7 . . . and eventually earn wealth and freedom!

Now that you are committed to handling anything that comes your way, you are ready to take on the world. But does the world know who you are? If they don't, that's *your* fault—and chapter 7 will help fix that problem.

Chapter 7

IF THEY DON'T KNOW YOU, IT'S YOUR FAULT

Why We Love It

We started doing "Why We Love It" Wednesdays on Facebook, where we highlight everything we love about being landlords.

Recently, we shared that we love it because of how we are able to help people. We received a call from a woman who was being abused by her ex-husband. She needed a place right away, but she had nowhere to go.

She had heard about our company, and she reached out. We worked with her to find a place where she could feel safe. We all ended that day with hugs and tears.

And that's why we're landlords!

Say My Name

Want another one of our investing secrets? It shouldn't be a secret that you're a landlord! You want people to know that you are an active real estate investor.

If people don't know you, it will make it a lot harder for you to buy new investment properties and for you to rent out those places to good tenants. We have people calling us almost every day, asking us to either rent them a place or buy their building. We are in constant contact with the right people.

But the right people aren't going to find you until you find them. And that's why you need to market yourself.

In this chapter, we will break down how to master marketing and deal with negativity.

Marketing Mastery

When we first started out, we'd walk or drive around and put flyers in people's mailboxes letting them know we wanted to buy their property.

And that did not work. We didn't get a single call. So we knew we'd have to think outside the box.

Here are some of the methods that have worked

well for us, whether through innovative marketing, on social media, or by networking. You can use any or all of these, depending on where you are in your growth and what your budget is.

Marketing 2.0

First things first: a website is a must. Come up with a company name (but consider not using your city, in case you want to expand later), and buy that domain. Then post pictures, videos, and descriptions so people can just go online and see your available units.

The next step we took was bold, but it works like magic: we placed ads on the radio in our city. Even though it's not cheap, it gets the word out *very* quickly. All of a sudden, people knew who we were. We have ads running all the time, saying things like, "Tired of being a landlord? We want to buy your rental property. Call Dupuis Properties." We keep it direct and to the point—and people know that we're active, serious, and motivated buyers. Now the cash cows come directly to us!

We advertise on huge billboards across the city and on our truck. Our logo is displayed on all our buildings. We also take out ads in a magazine that gets delivered monthly to targeted neighborhoods where other real estate investors live. These are big, bold, full-page, back-cover ads. Because of that, people call us first when they have properties to sell.

We want everyone to know about Dupuis Properties. We often hear, "You guys are everywhere!" Marketing lets us choose the best tenants and find the cream of the crop cash cows!

Social Media Marketing

Part of being everywhere all the time means having a strong presence online too. We are on everything: Facebook, LinkedIn, Snapchat, Twitter, Instagram, and YouTube. And we try to be interactive on most days.

You can be everywhere online too . . . and it's free!

Look at our "Dupuis Properties" and "Mel and Dave Dupuis—Real Estate Investors" pages on Facebook. Subscribe to our "Mel & Dave Dupuis—Real Estate Investors" YouTube page, and follow us on Instagram @melanddavedupuis. By doing so, you'll notice that most people like to share their opinions, so we often ask questions. As we were writing this book, we posted on social media asking people what they wanted to read about and what the book title should be. This ensured that we met the consumers' needs and created online interaction. Double win!

Social media can give you a huge advantage, because you have the opportunity to reach tenants *and* sellers. Be sure not to overlook it as one of the tools in your real estate investment tool belt.

Networking

Networking is part of marketing as well. This is where you get to meet people face to face and develop that personal connection. But you have to get out there and meet the people living and investing in your area.

Fundraisers and Chamber of Commerce meetings are great opportunities for networking. If your area has a landlord association, are you on it? Do you attend the meetings? This will give you access to information you didn't have before, because you are in a room full of other landlords. Ask them questions, and let them know that you want to buy properties.

When you attend meetings or events, go with the mission of meeting, shaking hands with, and talking with as many people as possible. Wear your uniform with your logo on it at all times, and hand out your business cards. Pretty soon, everybody will know you as the serious, successful, and *friendly* real estate investor you are!

Haters Gonna Hate

Now that everyone knows who you are and what you do, you'll inevitably hear from negative people and naysayers. We refer to those people as "haters."

Haters could be anyone: strangers, coworkers, acquaintances, and even sometimes friends and family. They aren't necessarily bad people or intent on putting you down. Most are simply either misinformed or just the type of person who is naturally negative.

But if you're not being talked about, you're not doing enough to create buzz. The more you put yourself out there, through your incredible marketing and networking, and the more people get to know you, the more you naturally open yourself up to the haters.

For some odd reason, from our own experience and from feedback received from other real estate investors, people give themselves the right to question your choice of investing in real estate. This can show up in many different forms. You'll hear, "Aren't you scared of the interest rates going up?" Or, "My uncle had his apartment wrecked by a tenant and lost thousands."

At first, it bothered us and even had us questioning if we were doing the right thing. But after years of hearing the same lines, we decided to just ignore what the haters say. So when (not if!) you start hearing those comments, don't let them stop you from achieving your cash-flow goals.

Adoring Fans

Let's be clear. Having haters doesn't mean that you're going to be hated. Some people may be jealous, unhappy for you, and overall naysayers. But you're going to have so many more fans than haters.

Strangers will adore you, admire you, encourage you, send you messages, and stop to talk to you in public. You're going to create such an awesome business and an amazing reputation that when the haters come along—especially if you're on social media—your fans are going to eat them up!

Of the thousands of people following us, commenting, liking, and sharing our posts, we've had just a few people post negative things. At first, we took it very personally, but then all of our other followers shut them down, and we saw what a great group of supporters we have around us!

Once people know your name, they're going to start calling. But how can you handle all the new tenants you're going to have and all the new buildings you will buy? You're going to need to build an elite team. Chapter 8 shows you that even the king of the jungle can't do it alone.

Chapter 8

EVEN THE KING OF THE JUNGLE CAN'T DO IT ALONE

Proud to Be Part of Dupuis Properties

Tommy, one of our amazing team members, is so proud to be a part of Dupuis Properties.

One day, he told us, "I heard your ad on the radio. I was playing my guitar this weekend, and I wrote a song for you guys. Maybe you can use it for your marketing."

All week long, Tommy gets calls for things to do with our tenants and buildings, and on the weekend, during his own time, he's still thinking of our team.

Tommy's a key player because he doesn't feel like he's working for us; he knows that he works *with* us.

Everybody Needs Somebody

Another secret to success? Surround yourself with people you can trust, because you can't do this alone.

At first, you may be able to handle a lot of it: maybe you clean units between tenants, make the dump runs, or do some of the repairs yourself. But if you want to continue to grow, you're going to need help. And as you grow more and more, you'll need more and more help.

If you look at landlords with five or six properties, they may still be handling most of the work themselves. But if you look at real estate investors who own fifteen or twenty properties, are they doing it all? Absolutely not, because it's just not feasible. If you do everything instead of hiring employees, you basically just created another job for yourself and put a ceiling on your growth capability.

Once we stopped doing everything ourselves and hired other qualified people to do it instead, we saw our rate of growth increase substantially. We see two reasons for this. One, it freed up our time to do what we wanted, which was finding and acquiring deals. Two, it became fun again, which increased our drive, rejuvenated us, and exploded our creativity and productivity.

Chapter 8: Even the King of the Jungle Can't Do It Alone   65

We're going to look at possible team members you may need, how to find them, and, once you do, how to keep them happy.

Who Do You Need?

You may already have some people on your team, or you may not have even thought about adding your first employee yet. Every situation is different, and everyone's needs are different. But you are going to need *someone* to help you and guide you.

First, you need a team of real estate investment-focused professionals.

This may include a realtor. Our realtor knows the deals that meet our criteria. He doesn't waste time sending us properties that he knows won't work for us. He understands and supports our various strategies for purchasing cash cows and will go above and beyond any time we need him to.

You'll also need help from a lawyer's office. Our lawyer understands how we acquire our properties and how we want to continue to grow our portfolio. We can walk in to meet with her any time, and she always makes time to answer our questions about a current deal or the next acquisition.

Other people to consider for your professional team include bookkeepers, accountants, bankers, mortgage brokers, private lenders, contractors, inspectors, and insurance brokers.

All this sounds pretty basic, but you need everyone you deal with to be top notch and to understand the ins and outs of real estate investing. Anyone can do your taxes, but if you find an investor-focused accountant, you can rest assured that you aren't missing out on any tax savings.

You will also want to build a team of people who work directly with you on your properties. This can include your maintenance team and service providers, such as plumbers and electricians.

But if you don't already have these people working for you, how can you find the right team?

How to Find the Right Team

You must ensure that the people you bring on board understand the real estate game.

How do you ensure this?

Pay attention and ask questions. Are they available for emergency calls? Can they handle dealing with various tenant interactions? How quickly do they return your calls and get the jobs done?

You want to look for people who care and want to grow with your business. Look for people who are personable, professional, trustworthy (remember that they will have keys to your tenants' homes), and skilled problem solvers. You don't want the people you hire to fix the problem to be calling you all the time with *more* problems. You want them to solve the issues so you can focus on growing your portfolio.

Just like we discussed for finding rentals and tenants, try to get the biggest pool of applicants possible. Use the various marketing tools discussed in the previous chapter to find them. We have found that, once we were well known, people came to us looking for employment. Our pool of applicants naturally increased.

And now we have the best team ever!

Keep Your Team Happy

Once you find those key employees, you will want to keep them on your team.

First, pay them well. The value they add to your organization, and the stress and pressure they remove from you, is worth every penny! You want your team to *want* to work with you long term because they love their work and feel valued. We make sure it's understood that the more they help us grow, the more we will increase their compensation.

However, it shouldn't be about just the paycheck. Give credit where credit is due. Praise your team on social media when they flip a unit, instead of taking credit for their hard work. Buy them lunch, thank them in person, and let them know that you appreciate them and the good work they do.

Provide your team with uniforms that *you* have purchased for them. Your team will go around the city proudly wearing your logo—a bonus for you.

We don't see ourselves as "the boss." We just see ourselves as part of a big team, and we try to portray that to our team members.

Ultimately, you have to spend your time focusing on what you love to do: investing in real estate.

Fun and Freedom

We love what we do. And right now, we manage all of our properties ourselves—with a lot of help from our fantastic team.

We don't plan to manage our own properties forever. If ever we find that it's no longer any fun and that we can't keep up, then we'll hire someone to do it if it makes financial sense to do so at that time.

We look at it as a win-win: we get to have fun and learn as we manage our properties now—while saving some money that we can use to buy more buildings—and we get to continue to grow.

That's our plan to have it all—fun, wealth, and freedom!

You are a *real* real estate investor, and you can create as much wealth and freedom as you commit to. In chapter 9, we'll show you how to take to the next level everything that you've learned throughout this whole journey.

Chapter 9

THE PERFECT TIME IS NOW

No Stopping Us

Investing in real estate has given us more opportunities than we could have ever imagined.

We bought our dream home and designed and installed an oversized inground pool. We drive the vehicles we want, take yearly winter family vacations, and, although we live in Northern Ontario, have taken the kids to Disney World three times. Melanie was also able to quit her full-time job and is now free from the typical Monday-to-Friday workweek.

But without real estate investing, none of that would have been possible.

If we had waited for the time to be perfect—when

we had enough money, when our kids were older, when we had more time—we never would have gotten started. Yes, we would probably be living in a nice house and driving good vehicles, but we would still be spending most of our time at work and living off a set budget.

Instead, we saw the joy on the girls' faces as they dressed up as princesses at the Magic Kingdom. We watched the three kids splash and play all summer in their new pool. We set the example that family always comes first. We have the gift of free time. And we come home to the house we always wanted, knowing that we are pursuing our passions and doing what we love together, every single day.

Create Your Vision

The most successful people in the world—Olympic athletes, actors, CEOs—use visualization to achieve their goals. That strategy, implemented with the help of vision boards, has changed our lives as well.

Our method may sound silly, but it's simple—and it works. You find what you want, print pictures of it, and put it on a vision board. Then you look at it and think about it as if it's already yours. It's as easy as you want it to be, and it's super powerful.

For example, Dave knew he wanted a wife just like Melanie after seeing her at the gym. Using the power of visualization, he focused on his goal, and years later, once the stars aligned, they officially met and have been together ever since.

One of the things Mel had on her first vision board was to own ten properties before she turned forty. That seemed like a pipe dream. But she's still not forty, and we have twenty-two properties so far—and are closing on more all the time!

Together, we created our own vision board with pictures of the dream vehicles, the dream vacations, and the dream house. When we were living in a tiny unit, driving around in our beater van, it all seemed so farfetched. But, with time, our vision boards were covered in checkmarks.

So then it became time to dream bigger!

As you accomplish your goals, you'll need to refresh your vision board—and that's the beauty of life. You keep extending, you keep reaching, because you may not even have realized what is possible for yourself, your life, and your family until you reach that next level.

Now and Forever

The number one thing that we had front and center on our first vision board together was financial freedom.

Mel was thankful to have a secure job with a great income, a pension, and benefits, but it wasn't what she wanted to do for the rest of her life. As we said earlier, that might be security, but it's not freedom.

By making enough rental income to replace Mel's salary, we can now check off that goal. Some people might say that three or four years is a long time to make all these sacrifices. But we spent three or four years focused on building our business—and that gave us a lifetime of financial freedom, time with our kids, and the ability to do what we love.

Our real estate portfolio now supports itself—and then some.

We don't plan to stop for the next twenty or thirty years: this is a passion, not a job. Everything we've created will eventually go to our kids. So, right from day one, we're able to give them wealth and freedom as well. They'll still have life lessons to learn, and they're not going to get a silver spoon, but it's nice to know that, no matter what, they're going to be okay. And someday, they may even pass it on to their kids, and the legacy we are currently creating will be passed on to create wealth for future generations.

Reach Out and We'll Reach Back

We are so grateful for our success, and it's important for us to give back, so we've become mentors to people who want to get started in real estate investing.

We want to help people who want to own five or ten properties. You may ultimately want to get to a hundred properties—and that's great!—but you have to take the first step and get to your first five, then ten, and so on. But don't do like Dave did and let fear of the unknown stop you!

If you are inspired but don't know where to start, please reach out to us. We know what it's like to get started, and we are more than willing to be your mentors. We have different training packages that we can create based on your needs. It doesn't matter if you're in our city or elsewhere—anything can be done long distance. We can guide you with as much or as little support as you'd like, whether that's reviewing a deal before you purchase it or customizing a plan for you.

The part we love most about what we do is working with people. Our main goal in life is to help people create freedom through real estate investing. And we hope that in a few years, you'll be where we are now—and then *you* can help other people who are just getting started. We can all be successful together. For more information regarding our mentoring programs, email us at realestateinvesting@dupuisproperties.com.

The Next Step Is Your First Step

What's your very next step? We have some action items for you to do today and within one week of reading this book. If you are already thinking that you can't do this *today*, then you are still finding excuses and waiting for the perfect time. But we want you to succeed, and that means putting things into action—*now*.

Task #1—Deadline: End of the day

- Reread the purpose that you wrote in chapter 1. (If you didn't take the time to actually do it when we first mentioned it, then do it now.)

- Write down your ultimate goal. Be clear and precise. Word it as if it's already been accomplished: "I purchased five properties this year," or "I net $10,000 a month."

- Write down what you want to put on your vision board.

Task #2—Deadline: One week from today

- Complete and post your vision board.
- Start creating your elite team. Research, find, and connect with a real estate agent, lawyer, accountant, and financial institution.
- Spend some time in self-reflection: How are you going to make more time to achieve your goal? What are you willing to cut out of your budget to ensure that you don't give the lenders a reason to say no?
- Make a to-do list for this month. What do you need to accomplish to get closer to your goal? How many properties will you crunch numbers on?

The Choice Is Yours

At the end of the day, you have two choices.

One is to stay where you are, to keep doing exactly what you're doing. You'll continue with the status quo.

But remember: you picked up this book for a reason. If our story lit a fire under you, then choose the second option: use that motivation to create the dream you want to live.

As you close this book, don't go do something else until you have taken that first action step.

Just start with the first step, and keep going. You can do it! You can achieve your goals, and wealth and freedom can be yours.

Ready?

Go!

ABOUT THE AUTHORS

Melanie and Dave Dupuis are experienced, successful, self-taught real estate investors taking the multi-family market by storm in North Bay, Ontario.

When they first met, Melanie and Dave's shared passion for real estate investing, their shared vision of financial freedom, and their understanding of what it would take to get there got this power couple set on the road to success. Although their shared passion and dedication have been the major drivers in their successful ventures, their eight years of education (which includes a marketing diploma and bachelor's degree in business administration) and career paths (including sales, marketing, higher education, emergency services, and civil service) were also instrumental in leading them toward their preferred future.

Melanie and Dave each had their own income properties before they met and ventured to integrate their commitment. Together, they founded Dupuis Properties and put their business plan into action. Their ultimate goal was to expand and to grow their real estate portfolio to a point where their investments became prosperous enough for Melanie to leave her full-time employment.

Their best year to date was when they impressively acquired twelve properties in less than twelve months. They currently own and manage twenty-two buildings and eighty-seven apartments. They have been recognized as one of the top three best rental property businesses in North Bay. And before turning forty, Melanie was able to quit her full-time job. This allows her to have the opportunity to focus her time on their real estate portfolio, while also enjoying wealth, freedom, and most importantly time with her three kids.

After such amazing success with Dupuis Properties, Melanie and Dave are also the founders and CEOs of a new company offering property management and repair and maintenance services to property owners and investors. They are also respected mentors. Melanie and Dave offer a variety of training programs to guide new and experienced real estate investors in building their own success.

They are ready and willing to share their secrets to help others build their own pathways to success and reach their own dreams.

WE'LL PUT YOUR MONEY TO WORK FOR YOU!

Want to invest in rental properties but don't have the time? Scared of investing with someone who doesn't have a proven track record?

Invest with us!

Our success, achievements, and tried-and-true method for investing with private lenders—along with our proven ability to repay on time and competitive interest rates—give you the best opportunity to put your money to work without the headaches.

Call Melanie and Dave at (705) 491-1058 or email realestateinvesting@dupuisproperties.com.

MENTORING PROGRAMS

Want to purchase rental properties but would like some one-on-one guidance?

We can provide you with an excellent opportunity to be mentored directly by us!

We offer a wide range of mentoring services based on your personal needs. Our mentoring programs will help you reduce your risks, avoid costly mistakes, and fast track your cash-flow success.

For more information regarding our mentoring programs, please email us at realestateinvesting@dupuisproperties.com.

Manufactured by Amazon.ca
Acheson, AB